Linking art to the world around us

Arty Facts
Light, Color
& Art Activities

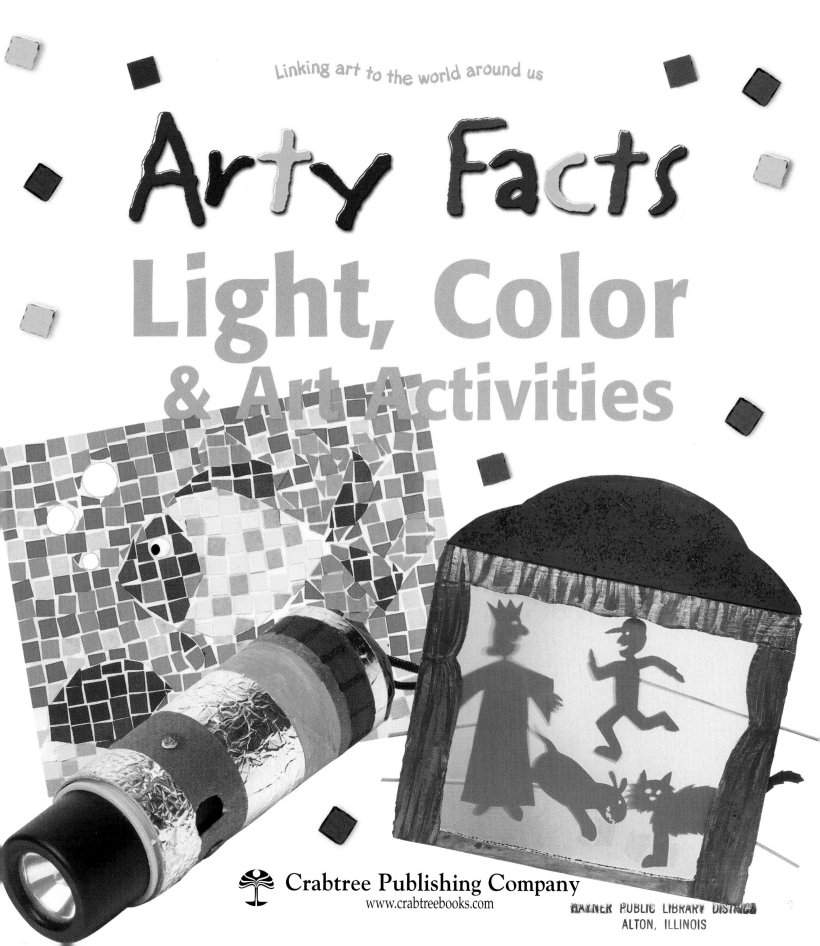

🌳 Crabtree Publishing Company

www.crabtreebooks.com

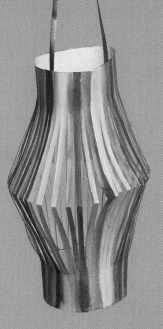

Crabtree Publishing Company

PMB 16A, 350 Fifth Avenue, Suite 3308
New York, NY
10118

612 Welland Avenue
St. Catharines, Ontario
L2M 5V6

Coordinating Editor: Ellen Rodger
Project Editor: Carrie Gleason
Production Coordinator: Rosie Gowsell

Project Development and Concept Marshall Direct:
Editorial Project Director: Karen Foster
Editors: Claire Sippi, Hazel Songhurst, Samantha Sweeney
Researchers: Gerry Bailey, Alec Edgington
Design Director: Tracy Carrington
Designers: Claire Penny, Paul Montague,
James Thompson, Mark Dempsey,
Production: Victoria Grimsell, Christina Brown
Photo Research: Andrea Sadler
Illustrator: Jan Smith
Model Artist: Sophie Dean

Prepress, printing and binding by Worzalla Publishing Company

Taylor, Barbara, 1954-
    Light, color, and art activities / written by Barbara Taylor.
        p. cm. -- (Arty facts)
    Summary: Information about various topics related to the science of light and
color forms the foundation for a variety of craft projects.
        Includes bibliographical references and index.
    ISBN 0-7787-1114-5 (RLB) -- ISBN 0-7787-1142-0 (PB)
        1. Color in art--Juvenile literature.   [1. Light. 2. Color. 3. Handicraft.]
I. Title. II. Series.
N7433.T238 2003
701'.85--dc21

                                                                2002011629
                                                                LC

Created by
Marshall Direct Learning

© 2002 Marshall Direct Learning

FRONT COVER IMAGES: SPECTRUM COLOUR LIBRARY; RICHARD HAMILTON-SMITH/ CORBIS; ROBERT HARDING PICTURE LIBRARY

Linking art to the world around us

Arty Facts

Light, Color & Art Activities

Contents

WRITTEN BY Barbara Taylor

Bright colors

Mixing colors

Primary colors are mixed in different combinations to produce almost all the other colors. When two primary colors are mixed together, the new color is called a secondary color. Red and yellow, for example, are mixed to make the secondary color, orange.

Printing primaries

Red, blue, and yellow are the primary, or basic colors most used by artists. In printing, another group of basic colors is used; magenta, a purplish-red color; cyan, a bluish-green color; and yellow. In both cases, the three basic colors produce many other colors when they are mixed together.

Shades, tints, and tones

If you combine the three primary colors, you get a color that is almost black. Darker blacks are produced by adding a powder called carbon black. Mixing black with a color creates a shade. Mixing white with a color creates a tint. Mixing gray with a color creates a tone.

When you look around you, especially on a sunny day, you see many different colors and different shades of color. Some flowers are red, the sky is blue, and the Sun is yellow. These three strong colors, red, blue, and yellow, are **primary colors**.

Light primaries

Different colors of light also combine to produce new colors. Red, blue, and green are primary colors in light. If you mix pure red and pure green light, you get yellow light. If you mix all three primaries you get white light, which appears to have no color at all.

Color

Choose strong colors for a really brilliant look!

WHAT YOU NEED

- gluestick
- ruler
- pencil
- scissors
- poster board
- construction paper

1 Using a ruler and pencil, draw small squares on sheets of colored construction paper and cut them out.

2 Sketch a design on poster board, then arrange the squares in a mosaic pattern.

3 Glue the squares to the poster board to complete your mosaic.

4 Use this method to make other pictures. Glue the colored construction paper into the different areas to color in your scene.

5

Sunshine

The Sun is the nearest star to Earth. It gives off light and heat because it is a whirling cloud of hot gases, which glows very brightly. Even though the Sun is 93 million miles (150 million km) from the Earth, light from the Sun reaches the Earth in only eight minutes! This is because light travels at an amazing 186,000 miles per second (300,000 km/s)!

Light for life

There would be no life on Earth without the light and warmth from our Sun. Plants use the Sun's light energy to make their own food. This process is called photosynthesis. Many plants, such as sunflowers, turn to face the Sun as it moves across the sky during the day.

Day and night

The Sun looks as though it moves up in the sky during the day and sinks down again at night, but it is really the Earth that is moving, not the Sun. The Earth spins around once every 24 hours. When your part of the Earth turns toward the Sun, it looks as if the Sun is rising and the day starts. When your part of the Earth turns away from the Sun, the Sun disappears and it becomes dark. The Earth spins eastward, which is why the Sun appears to rise in the east and set in the west.

Shadow clocks

Sundials were invented about 2,800 years ago in Egypt. As the Sun shines on a stick, called a gnomon, a shadow is cast on a dial marked in hours. As the Sun moves across the sky, the shadow moves around the dial, similar to the way hands move on a clock.

Sunflowers turn to face the light and warmth of the Sun

Light

WHAT YOU NEED

scissors

newspaper

pencil

glue

black pen

cardboard

tape

paints and brush

Golden sundial

1 Draw around a plate to make a circle on the cardboard. Cut it out.

2 Tear up strips of newspaper, and glue them all over the cut-out circle.

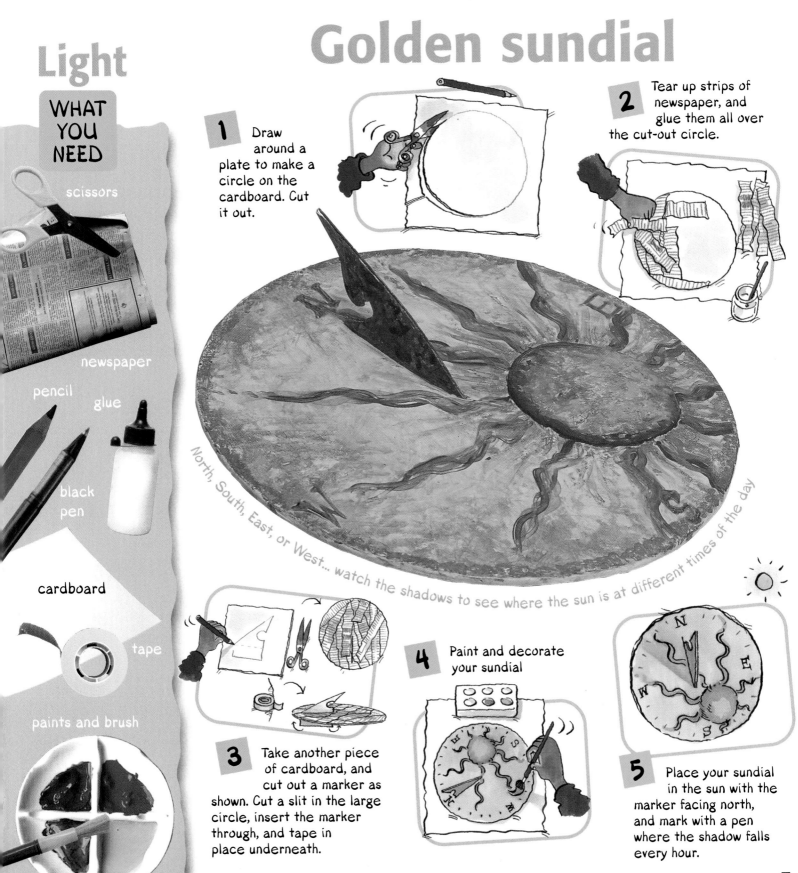

North, South, East, or West... watch the shadows to see where the sun is at different times of the day

3 Take another piece of cardboard, and cut out a marker as shown. Cut a slit in the large circle, insert the marker through, and tape in place underneath.

4 Paint and decorate your sundial

5 Place your sundial in the sun with the marker facing north, and mark with a pen where the shadow falls every hour.

7

Silvery shades

When you look down into a murky stream or river, it is difficult to see the fish that live there. Sometimes you spot a glint of sparkling silver, or a shadow gliding beneath the surface. The fish have special coloring that helps them to stay hidden from **predators**. The top sides of some fish are dark gray or green, while the bottom is white or silver. This coloring is a mixture of light and dark, called countershading.

Safety in numbers

A **shoal**, or school, of fish is made up of thousands of fish. Traveling together in a group gives small fish protection from predators. It is more difficult for a predator to single out and catch one fish swimming in such a large group.

Countershading in shoals

The shoal also uses light, shade, and color to protect itself from attack by bigger fish, such as sharks and stingrays. When the predator comes close by, the shoal turns away sharply. Sunlight sparkles on the silver sides of the fish, causing a sudden flash of light. This flash confuses the predator just long enough for the shoal to swim away. Other fish protect themselves from attack in different ways. Some are patterned or colored to blend in with their surroundings or the ocean floor. Some have sharp spines with poisonous tips growing from their sides or tail.

When a shoal of fish turns quickly, its sides flash silver to confuse predators.

Color

Flashing fish

Make a swimming shoal of silvery shining fish

WHAT YOU NEED

scissors

silver paper

pencil

double-sided tape

white poster board

string

black paper

wire

brush

black paint

silver paint

1 Fold a piece of poster board in half, draw a fish shape and cut it out. Do not cut along the fold.

2 Paint one side black. Cut circles from the silver paper and glue them on.

3 Using silver paint, paint a face and lines on the tail and fins.

4 Paint the other side silver and decorate with black circles and paint.

5 Stick the fish sides together using double-sided tape

6 Make a circle with the wire. Tie on four long pieces of string. Knot them together so that your mobile can hang from the ceiling.

7 Attach a piece of thread to the fish's fin. Tie the other end to the wire circle. Add more fish to your mobile.

9

Reflections

When you look in the mirror, you see a reflection of yourself. Light bounces off the mirror into your eyes, similar to the way a ball bounces off a wall. Reflections are caused by light bouncing off objects. Most objects reflect light in some way. Look at the picture below of the reflection of the Indian palace, the Taj Mahal, in the water. When the water ripples, the mirror image of the palace ripples.

Mirror Images

Mirrors produce very good reflections because they are smooth and shiny and reflect most of the light that shines on them. Mirrors are made of glass that has a reflective surface on the back. Your reflection in a mirror seems to be behind the mirror, but if you look behind the mirror, your reflection is not there!

Your image appears to be the same distance behind the mirror as you are in front of it. A mirror image is called a virtual, or unreal, image. Your reflection also reverses your true position, so that left and right are reversed. If you touch your right ear, your reflection touches its left ear and if you touch your left ear, your reflection does the opposite.

Curved mirrors

Curved mirrors change the size and shape of things reflected in them. A spoon is a sort of curved mirror. The front of the spoon curves inward. This is called a **concave** surface and it makes your reflection look upside down! The back of a spoon curves outward in a **convex** shape, so your reflection looks the right way up, but smaller. Fairground mirrors curve in and out to distort the reflections of people to make them look stretched out in some places and squashed in others.

Light

WHAT YOU NEED

paints and brush

sequins

newspaper   ball

glue

string

Mirror ball

1 Ask an adult to make a hole in the ball and attach a piece of string to it. Cover the ball with glue and strips of newspaper.

2 When the newspaper is dry, paint the ball a bright color.

3 Glue sequins of different sizes all over the ball until it is covered.

4 Hang it from the ceiling or in the window. Watch it catch the light and produce reflections.

Hang your mirror ball so it shines and reflects light. Brilliant!

Metallic gleam

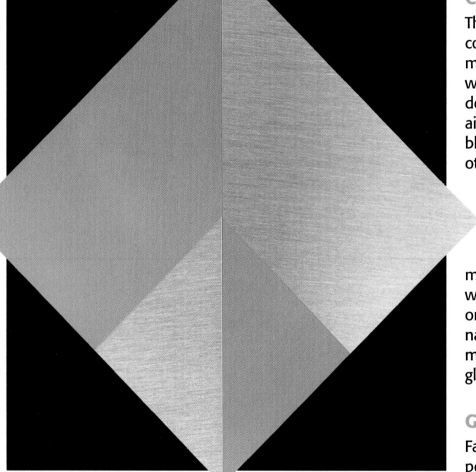

Changing colors

The color of gold stays the same, but the color of most other metals changes. The metal iron turns orangey-red with rust when it gets wet. Silver is polished, so it does not turn black when exposed to the air for a long time. To prevent silver from blackening, it is often mixed with other metals.

Shiny things

Many of the ordinary things we use every day are made of silvery, polished metals, such as steel or chrome. We also write messages with colorful metallic inks, or paint our nails with gleaming metallic nail polish. Cars are painted with a special metallic paint to give them a smooth, glossy shine.

Glittering stars

Famous movie actors or pop stars often perform on stage in gleaming, glittery, eye-catching outfits, made from colorful, metallic fabrics and shining metal jewelry. When we want a party or other celebration to be extra-special, we hang up silver and gold-colored decorations. We also give athletes gleaming gold, silver, and bronze medals as prizes at sports events, such as the Olympic Games.

Objects made from **metal**, or covered with a metallic coating, usually have a smooth surface, making them shine. The light reflects straight off the metal surface, quickly filling our eyes with light. A rough surface scatters the light, so less light reaches our eyes, making an object look dull. The metallic picture above has a variety of polished surfaces. These surfaces reflect light in different directions, resulting in a **geometric** pattern.

ANDY CRAWFORD

Color

Glitter lab

WHAT YOU NEED

paints and brush

bubble wrap

paper

poster board

sequins

scissors

straws

tin foil

silver and copper paper

cellophane

glitter

glue

1 Cut out and paint different shapes of tubes and glass beakers from poster board.

2 Line them up and glue them onto a piece of paper.

How many metallic textures will you add to your lab?

3 Glue straws, sequins, glitter, bubble wrap, and metallic papers onto the tubes and beakers.

PVA

Skylights

Far away from the **equator**, near the North and South **Poles**, a spectacular light show sometimes appears in the sky. This light show is called an aurora, which means dawn. Auroras are only seen at night, and appear as arcs, clouds, or streaks that move, brighten, or flicker across the sky.

Colored lights

Auroras are usually green, but those that appear very high in the sky may be red or purple. Most auroras shine 62 to 620 miles (100 to 1,000 km) above the Earth, and some stretch for thousands of miles.

Sky blue

Have you ever wondered why the sky is blue and sometimes other colors? It is because the different rainbow colors of sunlight – red, orange, yellow, green, blue, indigo, and violet – are scattered in all directions as they bounce off the dust and water **particles** in the Earth's **atmosphere**. Blue and violet light are easily scattered by the particles. Red light scatters the least. When you look at the sky on a clear day, you see a lot of scattered blue light, making the sky appear blue.

Painted sunsets

At sunrise and sunset, the Sun is low in the sky. The sunlight has to travel farther before it reaches us. Most of the blue color scatters out before it reaches your eyes. The red and orange light is what is left and it sometimes paints the sky with stunning colors.

Light

WHAT YOU NEED

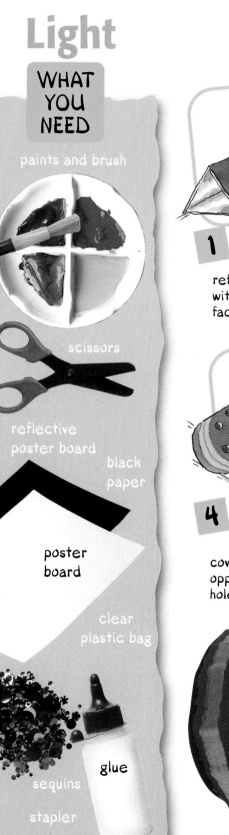

paints and brush

scissors

reflective poster board

black paper

poster board

clear plastic bag

sequins

glue

stapler

1 Make a long triangular shape from the reflective poster board, with the reflective side facing inward.

2 Make a tube from poster board that the triangular piece fits into. Paint and decorate with bright colors.

3 Put some sequins into a small plastic bag. Staple to close and glue to one end of the tube.

4 Insert the triangular piece into the tube. Cut a circle of black paper to cover the end of the tube opposite the sequins. Make a hole in the middle.

5 Glue the black paper over the end of the tube and trim it to fit. Shake and turn the kaleidoscope, and look through the hole in the end to see the different patterns it creates.

Twist and turn and watch the colors sparkle!

Flashing neons

Have you ever seen brightly colored **neon** signs lighting up a downtown street at night? These thin tubes of light are used on advertising signs and make a dazzling display. Neon lights are made using thin tubes that can be easily shaped into words and pictures. The tubes are filled with a gas that gives off a glow when **electricity** is sent through it.

The word neon comes from the ancient Greek word meaning new. When electricity travels through a glass tube filled with neon gas, it gives energy to the very tiny particles that make up the gas. As the electricity streams from one end of the tube to the other, it combines with the neon gas. This gives the neon particles more energy, just as a billiard ball is given more energy when it is hit by another billiard ball. The neon particles give out their new energy as a glowing light, which we see in the signs.

New energy

Neon is one of the gases found in the atmosphere, the mixture of gases that surrounds the Earth.

Color change

If the tubes are filled with other gases, different colored lights can be made. Neon gas gives out a strong orange-red glow. **Helium** gas gives a golden-yellow light, and **krypton** gas shines pale violet. When **sodium** vapor gas is used, it makes a vivid yellow light, which is often used in street lights.

Light

City lights

WHAT YOU NEED

paints and brush

gray poster board

glue

black poster board

tape

white pencil

scissors

1 Use the white pencil to draw two outlines of skyscrapers. Draw the tallest on dark gray poster board, and lower buildings on lighter gray. Cut them out.

2 Use paint to create lighted windows.

Brightly shining lights for a city that never sleeps!

3 Glue the tallest layer of skyscrapers onto a piece of poster board.

4 Fold the bottom of the lower row of skyscrapers and tape on top of the first layer, creating a 3-D effect.

17

Black and white

Reflect or Absorb

The color of the Earth's surface affects the way it reflects or absorbs the heat of the Sun. A white surface of snow or ice reflects about 90 percent of the Sun's heat. This makes snowy places, such as the Arctic and Antarctic, even colder than they already are. Black surfaces, such as a tar road, reflect only about five percent of the Sun's heat and absorb the rest. This is why dark paved roads get so hot on sunny days and even melt to form sticky tar. Animals that live in cold places, such as Arctic butterflies, often have dark colors to help them absorb heat from the Sun to stay warm.

Black and white are special colors. The squares on a chessboard are black and white to help separate them clearly. The black squares look so dark because black takes in, or absorbs, nearly all the colors in light. The white squares look so pale because white reflects all the colors in light.

Seeing in black and white

Did you know that many animals, such as dogs, cats, horses, and cows, cannot see the colors we see? They see the world in shades of black, white, and gray. Most people see in full color. Apes and monkeys also see in color. Other animals with color vision include reptiles, such as snakes and lizards, and birds, butterflies, bees, and many fish.

charcoal

white chalk

black and
white paper

poster
board

gluestick

Chalk and
charcoal designs

Make dramatic pictures by using only black and white

2 Use your finger
to smudge the
patterns in places.

1 Draw several pictures
using charcoal on white
paper, and chalk on black
paper. Draw big, bold,
unusual patterns using
your imagination!

3 Mount on
poster board

Make a display of
your chalk and
charcoal pictures.

19

Invisible rays

Sunlight brightens up the day. It also burns your skin if you are not careful. Visible light is light you can see, but the Sun also gives off light rays that you cannot see. The heat you feel from the Sun comes from invisible **infra-red** rays. A suntan, or worse, a sunburn, is from invisible **ultra-violet** rays.

Infra-red and ultra-violet light

When all the colors in a ray of sunlight are separated they make a rainbow of colors called a spectrum. The spectrum has a band of red at one end and a band of violet on the other end. Beyond each end of the spectrum are invisible rays of light. Infra-red means below red and ultra-violet means beyond violet.

Feel the heat

All hot things give off infra-red rays. The warmer something is the more infra-red rays it gives off. Special devices pick up infra-red rays and turn them into colors we can see. The hottest areas look yellow and the coldest areas look blue.

Dangerous rays

Ultra-violet, or UV, rays are dangerous because they pass through the outer layer of your skin and burn the flesh underneath. Too many UV rays cause a disease called skin cancer. A brown **pigment** called melanin, which turns skin brown, helps to protect skin from the harmful effects of ultra-violet rays.

A bee's eye-view

You cannot see ultra-violet light, but insects such as bees can. A bee's-eye view of a flower is very different from the view you see. The ultra-violet light reflected back from the flower makes it stand out more so the bee can find it easily.

This is how a bee sees a flower in ultra-violet light.

Light

WHAT YOU NEED

scissors

ribbon

poster board

paper

paints and brush

glitter

string

glue

Red and violet string print

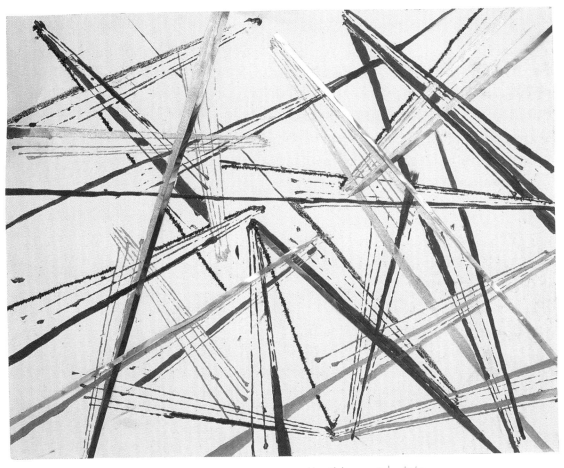

Make criss-cross patterns with ribbon and string

1 Cut long pieces of string and glue onto poster board.

2 Brush paint onto the string and then press the criss-cross patterns onto a piece of white paper.

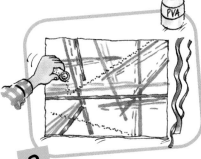

3 Add lines of glitter, paint, and pieces of ribbon to your string print picture.

21

I spy

The way we see a color is affected by the other colors around it. The same color looks lighter or darker when it is placed against a different colored background. For example, the central green square in the painting below stands out because it is framed by increasing shades of blue. If we change the colors around the central green square, the picture would look very different.

Seeing in color

Imagine you are eating a cheese and tomato sandwich. The cheese looks yellow because it reflects yellow light. The tomato looks red because it reflects red light. The other rainbow colors in light are absorbed by the cheese and the tomato so we cannot see them. We see different colors because of the way different objects reflect light. We see in color because of the millions of tiny cone-shaped **nerve endings,** called **cones**, at the back of our eyes. You have three types of cones, each respond to red, green, or blue light. Light from the cheese affects the green and red cones because mixing green and red light makes yellow light.

Color blindness

When something goes wrong with the cones in our eyes, the messages about light colors do not reach the brain. This causes color blindness. Color-blind people find it hard to tell the difference between certain colors, especially red, green, and gray.

Trick of the light

Puzzle pictures or **optical illusions** also trick the brain. Sometimes, what we think we see is not what is actually there. An illusion has two or more possible meanings. The brain cannot decide which one to choose, so we see one meaning and then another.

Color

Puzzle picture

1 Draw a small star in the corner of a piece of paper.

2 Draw some smaller shapes inside the star shape.

3 Cover the rest of the paper with more shapes.

4 Color in all the shapes with brightly colored paints.

Can you find the star hidden among the shapes?

23

Shadowy shapes

Have you ever played the "catch-my-shadow" game with your friends in which players chase each other's shadow? You need a sunny day for this game because your shadow only appears when your body blocks sunlight from reaching the ground.

Light rays

Light travels in straight lines called light rays. Light rays move in one direction as long as nothing is in the way of the path of light. When light rays hit an object, they are stopped. This leaves a dark space on the other side of the object called a shadow. On cloudy days, it is hard to see a shadow because the clouds soak up some of the sunlight and scatter the rest in all directions. All the sunlight has to move in one direction for a shadow to form.

Light and materials

Shadows form when light falls on materials that do not let the light pass through them. These are called **opaque** materials. Wood, metal, and your body are opaque. Other materials, such as air, water, and clear glass, let light travel through them. These materials are called **transparent**. Some materials, such as frosted glass, let a little light pass through them. These materials are called **translucent**.

In this play, dancing puppets cast shadows on a lit-up screen.

Light

WHAT YOU NEED

paints and brush

scissors

pencil

wood sticks

black paper

tape

tracing paper

glitter

cardboard box

Puppet theater

1 Cut out all four sides of the box to make a stage, as shown.

2 Paint red curtains at the front of the theater, and paint the sides and top using plain colors.

3 Cut a panel as shown. Paint and decorate it with glitter, then tape to the top of the theater.

4 Draw a variety of animal and people shapes on black construction paper and cut them out.

5 Tape the characters onto wooden sticks to make puppets.

6 Tape tracing paper to the inside front of the theater. Shine a light at the back of the box, and use the open sides to move your puppets.

The puppets' shadows will create a dramatic effect!

25

Laser beams

The most extraordinary light of all comes from a **laser**. Lasers punch through steel, carry telephone signals over long distances, are used by surgeons, play compact disks, read the bar codes at supermarket cash registers, and light up the sky with amazing patterns at a concert.

Light energy

A laser is a machine that produces a narrow beam of very bright light. Laser light does not scatter like ordinary light, so it is very powerful. It travels steadily in a direct path over long distances.

A laser light show at a rock concert.

Holograms

A hologram is a type of photograph that is made when two laser beams cross each other. It is made with light on glass instead of colors on paper like an ordinary photograph. A hologram looks like a 3-D solid object. If you walk around a hologram, it looks different from every angle, just like a real object does. Holograms look so real because they are accurate recordings of the light reflected from an object. Holograms are very difficult to forge, or copy, so they are used on credit cards, bank checks, and even concert tickets.

Light

Use your flashlight for night walks, camping trips, and slumber parties

WHAT YOU NEED

flashlight

cardboard tube

tin foil

paints and brush

scissors

tissue paper

sequins

glue

1 Cover the flashlight with a cardboard tube. Cut out a hole around the on/off button.

2 Paint and decorate the cardboard tube with strips of tin foil, tissue paper, and sequins.

PVA

3 Stuff the open end of the tube with ripped tissue paper to hold the flashlight in place.

27

Tints and dyes

Look at the clothes hanging in your closet. They are probably made of cotton, wool, nylon, or other different fabrics. Many of these fabrics are bright and colorful, with interesting patterns or designs, but almost all started as plain white material. All the colors and designs have been added by dyeing or tinting the fabric. A dye is a chemical that changes the color of something. A tint changes a color to a different shade.

Natural or synthetic

Dyes come from natural sources, such as the roots or berries of plants. Artificial, or synthetic, dyes were developed by scientists and are now used more than natural dyes. To work, the dye is usually dissolved in a dye bath full of a special liquid. When the fabric is added, its fibers absorb the tiny **molecules** of dye and it changes color. To stop the color from fading, a substance called a **mordant** is added. The mordant combines with the dye molecules to fix them permanently into the fabric to make the material **colorfast**.

Color

Experiment to create different tie-dye patterns

WHAT YOU NEED

newspaper

white or pale colored T-shirt

rubber bands

cold water dye

old bowl or bucket

rubber gloves

scraps of fabric

1 Spread out newspaper to protect the work area. Wrap rubber bands around sections of a T-shirt.

2 Make the dye in a bowl or bucket. Follow the instructions on the package. Wearing rubber gloves, put the T-shirt in the dye.

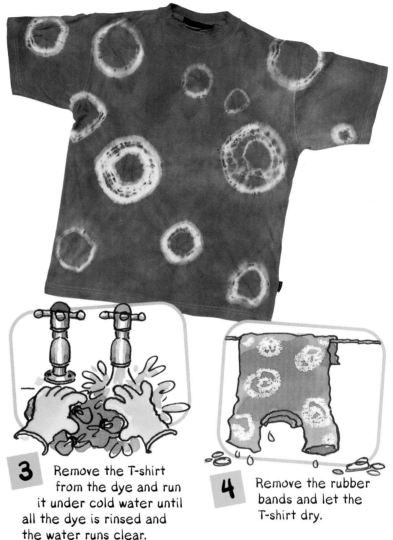

3 Remove the T-shirt from the dye and run it under cold water until all the dye is rinsed and the water runs clear.

4 Remove the rubber bands and let the T-shirt dry.

You can create different patterns by wrapping the rubber bands in different ways. Experiment on scraps of fabric to get the effect you want. You can also try:

* scrunching the fabric
* knotting the fabric
* folding the fabric

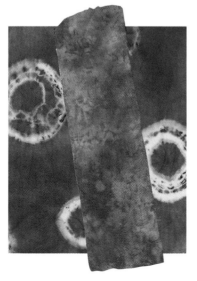

Tie-dyeing can be messy so ask an adult to help

29

Dots and pixels

A close-up of pixels on a television screen.

If you look at the picture on a color television screen really closely, you see that it is made up of many red, blue, and green dots. There are about 350,000 of these dots, called pixels, or picture elements. From a distance, the dots merge together so they look like one picture in full color.

From camera to screen

A color television camera converts the picture it captures into electrical signals. These signals are then changed into **radio waves**, which are sent through the air to the television set. The television set works in the opposite way to the television camera, changing the radio waves first into electrical signals and then into a pattern of colored light. This pattern is the picture you see on your television screen.

Mixing light

All the colors you see on a television screen are made by mixing red, blue, and green light. These are the primary colors of light. Light colors do not mix in the same way as paint colors. Red and green light mix to make yellow. Blue and green light make cyan, a bluish-green color. Red and blue light make magenta, a purplish-red color. All the colors of light mixed together make white. What color do you get if you mix the primary colors of paint: red, blue, and yellow, together?

Splitting and mixing

A television camera splits the light from an image into the three primary colors. Each color goes to a different camera tube, which converts the light into electrical signals. Inside a television is an **electron gun** with three tubes, one for each primary color. The gun fires electrical signals at the back of the television screen, which is coated with strips of chemicals called **phosphors**. When the electrical signals come in contact with the phosphors, they glow red, green, or blue to make the color picture.

Light

WHAT YOU NEED

powder paints

brush

white paper

acrylic paints

pencil

poster board

Spot painting

Mix colors and make pretty patterns in this dot collection!

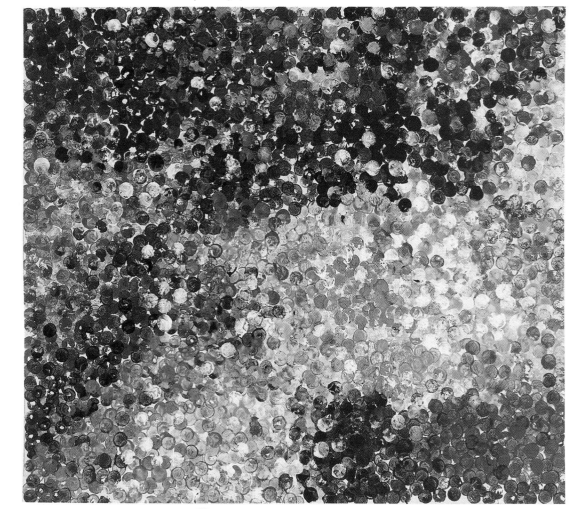

1 Dip the end of the pencil into different kinds of colored paints and press them onto white paper.

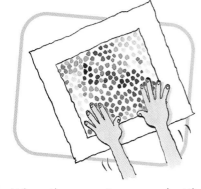

2 When the page is covered with dots, leave the picture to dry and mount it on poster board.

31

Floating bubbles

H ave you ever tried to blow bubbles? Soap is needed to make bubbles. You need the soap to make the water particles stretch apart enough to form a bubble. The soap particles help stop the water in the bubble from escaping and the bubble from bursting. A bubble expert once kept a bubble for 340 days, but most bubbles pop much sooner than that!

Bubble shapes

Bubbles are usually rounded shapes called spheres. The particles that make up the bubble liquid stick together. When bubbles meet, their liquid skins stretch and bind together, minimizing the **surface area**. The merging of the bubbles creates a sphere shape. A sphere has a smaller surface area than other shapes, such as cubes and cylinders.

Bubble colors

One of the most beautiful things about bubbles is their shimmering rainbow colors. These colors come from the way light reflects from the inner and outer surfaces of the bubbles. Light reflected from the inside of the bubble travels a longer distance than the light reflected from the outside of the bubble. When the inside and outside reflections meet, the different colors in the light interfere with each other, creating the colored patterns. These are called **interference colors**.

Light

WHAT YOU NEED

poster board

white paper   straw

paint

dish soap

spoon

bowl

1

In the bowl, mix together a small amount of water, dish soap, and a squirt of paint.

2 Blow into the mixture through the straw, creating colored bubbles.

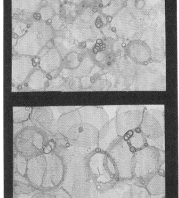

3

Lay a piece of paper over the top of the bowl and skim it across the bubbles.

When dry, mount your pictures.

4

Blow bubbles, and see amazing patterns appear!

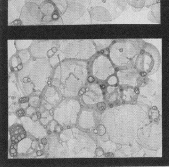

33

Firecrackers

Bang! Whizzzz! Whooop! Fizzz! The sky is suddenly filled with bright patterns of colored light as rockets explode high overhead. Pinwheels whirl around, throwing out showers of sparkling stars, and golden and silver rain cascades to the ground. Where do all the fantastic colors in fireworks come from?

Burning-metal effects

Firework colors are produced when different metals burn, creating different colored flames. **Magnesium** metal makes a brilliant white light when it burns. Sodium burns with a yellowish-orange color. **Copper** and **barium** give off a bluish-green color. **Lithium** and **strontium** burn red, and **potassium** makes fireworks violet.

Rocket science

Firework rockets are packed with gunpowder. When gunpowder is packed tightly into a thin tube, it burns very quickly and is super hot. As the gunpowder burns, smoke and hot gases stream from the bottom of the rocket and push the rocket up into the sky. A long stick attached to the tube keeps the rocket flying in a straight line. Eventually, the burning powder sets fire to an explosive charge that makes glowing shapes shoot out the end of the rocket. Sometimes, the gunpowder is mixed with chemicals and packed in separate layers, so that as each layer explodes, it releases a different color.

Color

Firework display

WHAT YOU NEED

silver and gold paint

black paper

paintbrush

glitter

glue

pastels

1 Make small dots with pastels on the paper and smudge them with your finger.

2 Add spots of silver and gold paint. Spread on glue in swirls and sprinkle with glitter.

Add swirls of glowing paint to make your display shine in the dark

Color and mood

Colors affect us in many ways. They change our mood, or the way we feel. Red, orange, and yellow are warm colors that make us feel cheerful and excited. The sun glows yellow and orange. Blues and greens are cool colors, which give us calm, secure feelings. People cool off in the shade of green trees or go for a refreshing dip in the blue-green ocean.

Decorating colors

The colors people choose when they are decorating their homes changes the feel of the rooms. Pale shades of cool colors, such as pastels, make rooms feel spacious and peaceful, while warm colors make rooms feel friendly and cozy. Dark colors have a shrinking effect, making rooms appear smaller and high ceilings feel lower.

Colors and food

How would you feel if you had to eat blue rice or purple pizza? The color of our food is almost as important as its taste. Some frozen or canned foods have artificial color added to them so we will want to eat them. The color of food often tells us whether it will be good to eat. Fresh vegetables are green, while old vegetables turn yellow and brown.

Artists use different colors to change the mood of the viewer. How does this painting make you feel?

Color

Soft-glow lampshade

WHAT YOU NEED

gold paint and brush

wire

craft knife
(ask an adult for help when using a knife)

poster board

scissors

tissue paper

glue   tape

1 On poster board, draw a big circle with a smaller circle in the middle. Cut it out.

2 Cut out shapes with a craft knife. Then paint the frame of the lampshade gold.

This colorful lampshade will give your bedroom a warm and cozy feeling

3 Glue strips of different colored tissue paper on the inside of the lampshade. Trim the tissue paper so that a different color shows through each hole.

4 Bend the two ends of the shade around so they are joined and tape together.

5 Make a wire circle, with a straight piece across the middle, as shown. Attach this to the top of the lampshade. Ask an adult to hang it from the light.

Rolls of film

Smile, please! Taking pictures is fun and it is nice to have photographs to remind you of special events, people, and places. Photography means "writing with light" and a photograph is a copy of a pattern of light that you can look at again and again.

How a camera works

A camera works the same way as your eyes do. The camera has a lens that collects all the light from a scene and bends the light so that it falls on the film to form a picture, or image. Both the eye and a camera control the amount of light that goes into the image. The camera controls light by changing the size of a hole, called the **aperture**, and the amount of time a flap, called the **shutter**, stays open to let light into the camera.

Developing and printing

When you have taken all the pictures on a roll of film, they are turned into prints. The film is dipped in **chemicals** that make it less sensitive to light. These chemicals make the light colors on the film appear dark and the dark colors appear light. The developed film is called a negative because it is a reverse of the real image. To make the print, light is shone through the negative onto special paper. When the light hits the chemicals on this paper, the light and dark areas of the negative are turned back to their real color on the paper.

Light

WHAT YOU NEED

scissors

black paper

black paint

pencil

gluestick

tracing paper

yellow paint or ink

Cartoon snapshots

Make negatives of your own special scenes

Glue the tracing paper onto the back of the black frames to create your film.

1 Make several film frames from black paper. Cut holes along the sides, as shown, so the frames look like film.

2 Brush yellow paint or ink onto sheets of tracing paper.

3 Use black paint to create images on the yellow background.

39

Magic glass

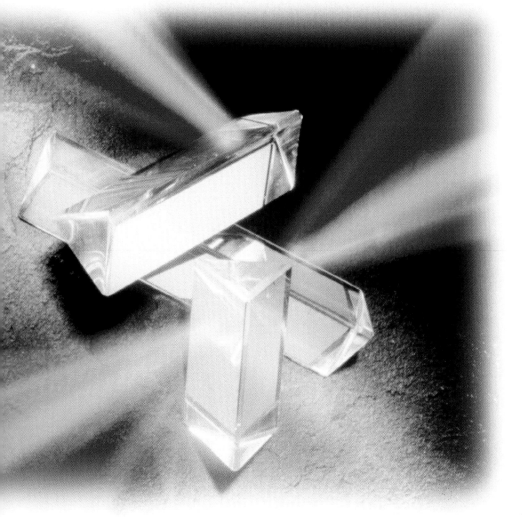

Newton's prism

Newton suggested that the prism had split the light into red, orange, yellow, green, blue, indigo, and violet light. Most other scientists during Newton's time thought that the prism added something to the light to make the colors. Newton showed that sunlight is really a mixture of different colored lights.

Color paths

When light travels through a prism, each of the colors moves at a slightly different speed. This makes the path of each color bend a different amount. As the colors leave the prism, each one follows a different path, so each color is separate. If the colored light passes through a second prism, the colors are bent back together again so the light shining out of the prism has no color. This is called white light.

Bending light

Light always travels in straight lines. When light goes through water or glass, it appears to bend. Bending light is called **refraction**. The light slows down when it hits the water or glass. This makes the light change direction, and move at a different angle, so it looks as if it is bending.

More than 300 years ago, a scientist named Isaac Newton did experiments with light. He held a thick triangle of glass, called a prism, in front of a thin beam of sunlight. He put some white paper in front of the prism and saw a rainbow of colors, called a spectrum, shining onto the paper.

TECMAP CORPORATION/ CORBIS

Light

Make a model prism, and see all the colors of light

WHAT YOU NEED

wire

bubble wrap

cellophane

tissue paper

tin foil

tracing paper

glue

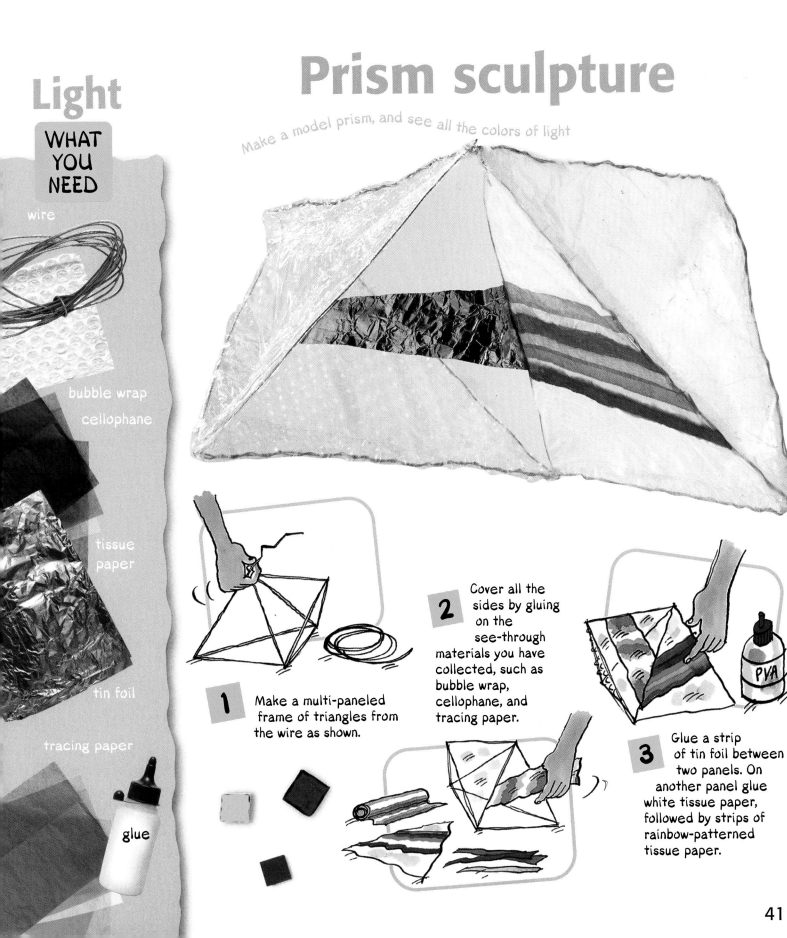

1 Make a multi-paneled frame of triangles from the wire as shown.

2 Cover all the sides by gluing on the see-through materials you have collected, such as bubble wrap, cellophane, and tracing paper.

3 Glue a strip of tin foil between two panels. On another panel glue white tissue paper, followed by strips of rainbow-patterned tissue paper.

Clear crystals

Glittering and sparkling in the light, the smooth, shiny sides of clear crystals reflect all the colors of the rainbow. Crystals are a variety of shapes, sizes, and colors, but they all have a repetitive pattern of flat surfaces and angles. Crystals form naturally underground, in the rocks beneath the Earth's surface.

Minerals

Our whole planet is built from minerals. Minerals are natural, non-living materials. Some minerals are precious and rare, such as diamonds. Other minerals, such as quartz, are found almost everywhere.

Earth's rock jewels

All minerals form in magma, which is the hot, molten rock under the Earth's surface. Most minerals have crystal shapes. There are six basic crystal shapes and most crystals have a specific color. Many **gemstones** are crystals that have been cut and polished. Rare gems, such as rubies and emeralds, are very precious.

Prisms and pyramids

Crystals form into prism shapes, with flat, smooth, shiny sides and sharp corners. Sometimes the prisms have flat ends, and other times they have pyramid-shaped ends. Quartz always forms crystals with six-sided prisms and six-sided pyramid ends. Salt always forms cube-shaped crystals. Some crystals are so perfectly shaped, they look as if a machine has cut them, but they are completely natural!

Colors and light

Crystals such as pure quartz are clear and colorless. When another material mixes with a forming crystal it colors it yellow, purple, pink, or brown. Colored crystals are very beautiful and are often used in jewelry. We call crystals like these gemstones.

Color

WHAT YOU NEED

sequins

tin foil

buttons

nylon

cellophane

tracing paper

beads

scissors

gold thread

wire

Quartz mobile

Hang your shining crystal by the window so it reflects the light

2 Wrap the wire with twisted pieces of foil.

1 Make a frame from the wire, as shown.

Attach these pieces to the top of your crystal so they dangle down the middle.

3 Use a needle to thread sequins, buttons, and plastic beads onto pieces of gold thread or nylon.

4

5 Cover the sides with cellophane and tracing paper, then decorate the outside with sequins.

PVA

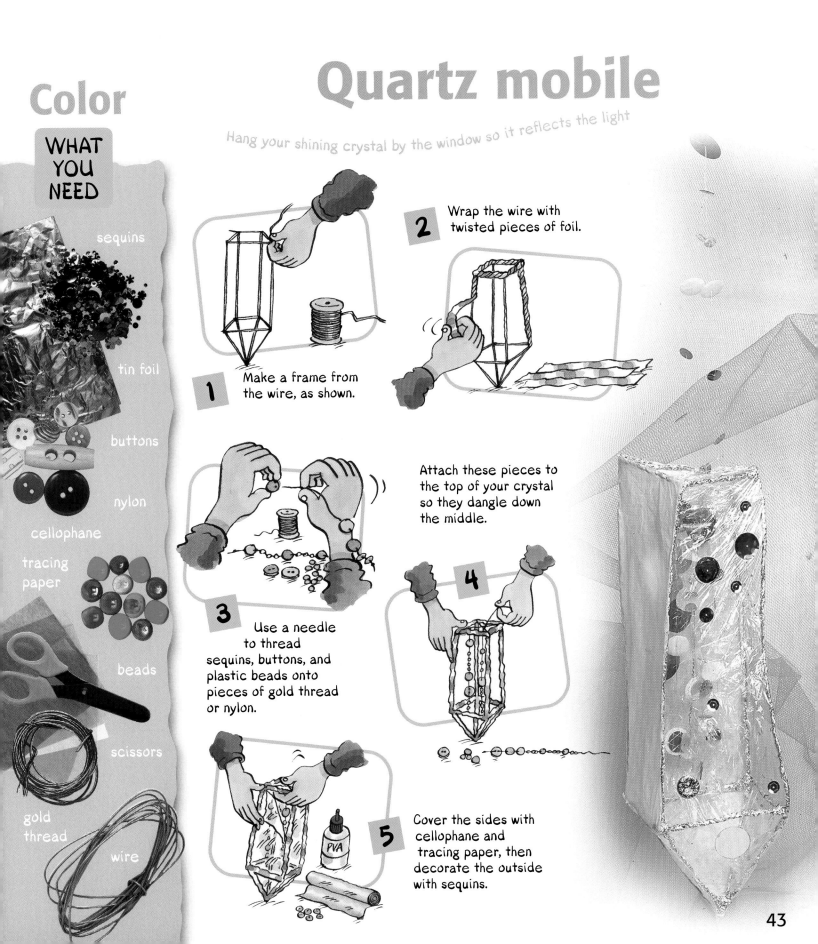

43

Lamps and lanterns

All over the world, light and color are an important part of festivals. In some cultures, lamps and lanterns guide visiting goddesses, welcome the spirits of the dead, or remind people of events that happened long ago. Colors make occasions, such as the coming of Spring, New Year, or independence days, even more special.

Festival of lights

In late October or early November, people of the Hindu religion celebrate the Festival of Lights, called Diwali. Before sunset, people set out rows of Diwali lamps outside their front doors, on windowsills, or on rooftops. Diwali means "row of lights." Hindus believe that the lights help to guide the goddess Lakshmi, who brings good luck to the family in the house for the next year.

Welcoming lanterns

Japanese Buddhists celebrate the Festival of Bon, also called the Festival of Lanterns, every July. The festival remembers those who have died by placing a lighted lantern at the door to welcome the spirits into their homes. On the last day, people light paper lanterns, and set them on wooden rafts in the water. As they drift into the dark, the tiny lantern boats light up the waters and carry the spirits to the other world.

Light

Chinese lanterns

WHAT YOU NEED

paints and brush

sequins

tape

paper

scissors

glue

string

1 Fold a piece of paper in half lengthwise.

2 Cut slits along the fold.

3 Unfold the paper, then paint and decorate with sequins.

Tape the two outer edges of the paper together to create a cylinder shape. **4**

5 Tape a piece of string inside the top of the lantern to hang it up.

Hang your lanterns all around the house to make it look cheerful and festive

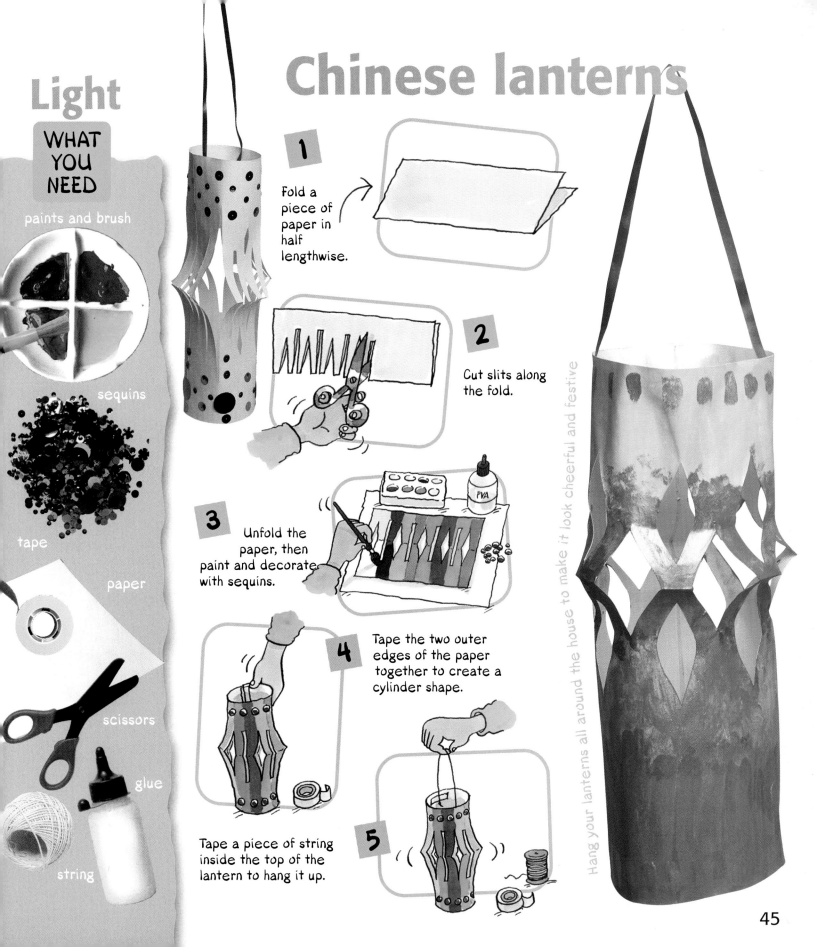

45

Glossary

aperture The hole in the lens of a camera through which light enters.

atmosphere The layer of gases surrounding Earth.

barium A soft, white metal.

chemicals Substances produced by or used in chemistry.

colorfast Color that will not run when washed.

concave Curving inward.

cones The cells in the back part of our eyes which detect light and color.

convex Curving outward.

copper A metallic element that is reddish-brown.

electricity A natural form of energy that can also be produced to power lights and other electronic devices.

electron gun A device in the back of the television set that shoots out a stream of electrons, or negatively charged particles that carry electricity.

equator The imaginary line around the center of the Earth that divides Earth into the northern and southern hemispheres.

gemstone A mixture of quartz and other colored materials which can be mined from the Earth.

geometric Simple shapes made up of simple lines or curves.

helium A colorless, odorless gas that is very lightweight.

infra-red Invisible rays given off by the Sun.

interference colors Colors made when light waves of different lengths mix with each other.

krypton A gas that is used in fluorescent lights.

laser A device which sends a narrow beam of light in one direction.

lithium A highly reflective metallic element.

magnesium A silvery-gray metal found in many minerals and in sea water.

metal A hard, and usually shiny substance.

molecule The most basic unit of matter.

mordant A substance which can be added to dyes to make them stay in the material.

neon A colorless gas found in the atmosphere.

nerve endings The tips of nerves, or bundles of specialized cells, that perform specific tasks, such as detecting light or touch.

opaque Describes an object or material that is not transparent and does not transmit or reflect light.

optical illusions False messages sent to the brain by the eye.

particle A name for a very small part of a substance. Atoms and electrons are particles.

phosphors A substance which glows with light when it is charged with electricity.

pigment A substance that gives color to something.

Poles The northernmost or southernmost point on Earth's axis. Earth's axis is the imaginary line running through the center of the planet on which the Earth rotates.

potassium A soft, silvery metal.

predators Animals that hunt and kill other animals for food.

primary colors The colors red, blue, and yellow, which can be mixed to make other colors.

radio waves Invisible waves of energy through which sound messages travel.

refraction The bending of a light ray or sound wave as it passes from one substance to another.

shoal A school of fish or other marine animals.

shutter A mechanism used in cameras to control how much light can enter.

sodium A silver white element of many metals.

strontium A soft, silvery-white metal.

surface area The size of the entire outer part of an object.

translucent Describes an object or material that is semi-transparent, or allows light to partially pass through it.

transparent Describes an object or material that is see-through, or allows light to pass through it.

ultra-violet Invisible rays from the sun.

Index

Materials guide

The crafts in this book require the use of materials and products that are easily purchased in craft stores. If you cannot locate some materials, you can substitute other materials with those we have listed here, or use your imagination to make the craft with what you have on hand.

Gold foil: can be found in craft stores. It is very delicate and sometimes tears.

Silver foil: can be found in craft stores. It is very delicate, soft and sometimes tears. For some crafts, tin or aluminum foil can be substituted. Aluminum foil is a less delicate material and makes a harder finished craft.

PVA glue: commonly called polyvinyl acetate. It is a modeling glue that creates a type of varnish when mixed with water. It is also used as a strong glue. In some crafts, other strong glues can be substituted, and used as an adhesive, but not as a varnish.

Filler paste: sometimes called plaster of Paris. It is a paste that hardens when it dries. It can be purchased at craft and hardware stores.

Paste: a paste of 1/2 cup flour, one tablespoon of salt and one cup of warm water can be made to paste strips of newspaper as in a papier mâché craft. Alternatively, wallpaper paste can be purchased and mixed as per directions on the package.

Cellophane: a clear or colored plastic material. Acetate can also be used in crafts that call for this material. Acetate is a clear, or colored, thin plastic that can be found in craft stores.

WHAT YOU NEED

gold foil

silver foil

filler paste

PVA glue

flour

salt

cellophane or acetate

 1 2 3 4 5 6 7 8 9 0   Printed in the USA   0 9 8 7 6 5 4 3 2